Copyright 2006 by Lawrence Crane Enterprises, Inc.

All rights reserved. No part of this book may be reproduced or transmitted in any form or by any means, electronic or mechanical, including photocopying, recording, or by an information storage retrieval system, without permission in writing from the publisher.

Publisher:
    Lawrence Crane Enterprises, Inc.
    15101 Rayneta Drive
    Sherman Oaks, CA 91403
    Phone: 888-333-7703 or 818-385-0611
    Fax: 818-385-0563
    Email: ReleaseLA@aol.com
    Web site: www.releasetechnique.com

ISBN No. 0-9778726-0-2

Printed in the United States of America

Library of Congress number TX5-021-629

The publisher and author of this material make no medical claims for its use. This material is not intended to treat, diagnose or cure any illness. If you need medical attention please consult with your medical practitioner.

The Power of Love

Learn how to be in the now

by Lester Levenson

Love is the most powerful force in the universe

FOREWORD

"The only method of receiving love is to give love, because what we give out must come back."

Lester Levenson was born in Elizabeth, New Jersey, on July 19, 1909.

Lester sailed through school and college with astonishing ease, becoming a physicist, an engineer, a successful businessman and a self-made millionaire. Yet despite all his achievements there was an innate turmoil in his heart, an anxiety and stress that seemed to rule his life.

In 1952, at the age of 42, Lester had his second massive heart attack. In those days, they did not have bypass surgery or heart transplants and so when he came out of the emergency room, the doctors told him, "Lester, we're sorry to tell you, but you have two weeks to live, three at the most, and we can't do anything for you. So we're sending you home."

So Lester went home.

Being a physicist, he knew he had to go back to the drawing board, wipe the slate clean, and start from point zero. So he started to examine his life. He noticed that each time he was ill he was wanting something and that the intense wanting feelings were what was actually making him miserable. He wanted love, he wanted money, he wanted to change things, and every time he looked at that wanting, he had an uncomfortable feeling that he traced back to his illness. Then he noticed that whenever he was giving and loving and wasn't wanting anything, he was not ill. So, he asked himself, "Well, if I could get rid of all my non-loving feelings, would I get better?" He thought about this question and uncovered something that was startling to him at the time.

He noticed that when he was loving he was happiest. That happiness equated to being loving rather than being loved.

> *HE NOTICED THAT WHEN HE WAS LOVING HE WAS HAPPIEST. THAT HAPPINESS EQUATED TO BEING LOVING RATHER THAN BEING LOVED.*

That was a starting point. He asked himself if he could cure his illnesses this way. So, he began connecting all of his thoughts and feelings in that direction—from that of "wanting to be loved," to that of "loving." He examined all his relationships and he let go of all of his non-loving feelings from the past. In that process he made another shocking discovery: He saw that he wanted to change the entire world and that was the cause of all his ailments, making him a slave to this world. He decided to reverse that by actually unloading the subconscious concepts and pressures, and by taking responsibility for everything happening in his life. At this point he discovered that limitations were only concepts in our minds and can easily be dropped. He realized that God is within us all, that we are infinite beings with no limitations. With that realization, he became happier: freer, lighter and with an overall sense of well-being.

Later on he would say: "We are all gods acting like goddamned fools."

Months went by and Lester still wasn't dead. He hardly went to sleep, he ate a little bit, and he continued to work on himself. He corrected his physical body. All of his miseries dropped away and he found himself in a place in which he was happy all the time, without sorrow. He totally cured himself.

More than that, Lester unlocked the science of the mind: How the mind works, what to do about it and how to correct it. How to correct your thinking. How to call up the menu of your mind, take a look at this menu and eliminate what you don't want.

Lester was a giving person—one thousand percent! He spent the remainder of his life helping others discover this secret that he had unlocked for himself. He passed on in 1994 at the age of 84—42 years after being told he had two to three weeks to live!

And before he died, he asked me to continue his work.

The Power of Love

My name is Larry Crane. I was born in the Bronx. I grew up in a poor family. We never missed a meal, but I thought the rich man lived on the top floor and the poor man lived in the basement. And we lived in the basement. As a young boy, I had many, many jobs; I was very aggressive. I worked hard, put myself through New York University, The Leonard Stern School of Business, and when I graduated college in 1957, my father told me if I could make $100 a week, it would be a terrific accomplishment. I noticed some of my friends who graduated started to be successful and were making lots of money, so I said to myself, "I'm just as smart as they are. I can do that, too." So I went about life and business in a very aggressive way, like "Get outta my way—I'll take what I want—I'm gonna have what I want or I'll knock you down." And in time, I climbed my way to the top.

During that period I got married and had twin sons but never made any time for them. I started in the advertising business and quickly became the advertising and marketing director of Remco Toys. After a few very successful years, I started my own direct mail business, Telehouse, Inc., which was the

The Power of Love

first of its kind to sell record packages on television. The company quickly became very successful. We started to make millions of dollars. I divorced my first wife and married a beautiful, beautiful woman. I bought a ten-room duplex penthouse in Manhattan. I had the limousines, the planes—I had businesses all over the world making multi-millions. Yet, I was absolutely miserable!

It was quite confusing to me. One night I came home to my fabulous ten-room Manhattan penthouse apartment. Time magazine had written an article about me, and the doorman greeted me with, "Mr. Crane, what an honor to have you in my building. For me to take you up to your penthouse is my pleasure." This was a Friday night around 9 p.m. and I remember getting out of the elevator and being so unhappy and so miserable that I actually walked over to the terrace and for about two hours I contemplated jumping—ending it all. I call this the second greatest day of my life! (The first: Meeting Lester Levenson). But that Friday evening I, too, examined my life. I asked myself what am I doing on the planet? What is life about? I observed that I did not know what I was doing on

Earth, but for me life was only about making money. I was so focused on money that I did not even allow myself to spend much, enjoy much or do much with it. That was confusing. I decided that evening to find an answer. After all, I had no reason to be miserable: I had millions of dollars, a beautiful wife, a fabulous business, businesses all over the world, media attention, and so on and so forth. Still, I was miserable. I was not interested in drugs or drinking. These things had no appeal to me and thank God I never turned in that direction. Since I was not willing to jump and end it, I needed to find an answer.

At the time, I was not receptive to psychiatric work. I was not open to transcendental meditation or yoga. I was pretty closed in those days and yet I wasn't willing to jump. So I became determined to find an answer. What that answer was, I did not know. My wife at the time talked me into some New Age courses, which I took, but I still found no answer after taking a number of them and trying to put an end to my unhappiness. I tried and tried, but I did not have the answer that I wanted. All I really wanted was to get out of my misery. I discovered I was angry. I discovered I had fear. I discovered I was doing things that were destructive and not quite intelligent behavior, yet I didn't know what to do about it. None of the courses showed me what to do about it. I just became more and more frustrated. I then took some additional courses, but still to no avail.

Then one day, in 1976, a man came into my office to sell me a mail order item. I had some interesting spiritual or self-discipline quotations on my office wall which often opened up a conversation of what I was into and the answers I was seeking. This salesman told me about "The Release® Technique." It really resonated with me, so I decided to take the course that very weekend. That same weekend, I met Lester Levenson, my mentor, my teacher, who I was fortunate enough to know for twenty-two years. I spoke to him almost every day, many times during the day. I took trips with him around the country and was quite fascinated by his clarity, his calmness and his givingness.

Now let's talk about what people are looking for— what everyone is looking for—and how to get it.

Everyone is looking for "happiness with no sorrow" or peace of mind, but most people are looking for this outside themselves. They are looking for it in someone, in some thing, in making money, being a big shot, having possessions. Unfortunately, it is impossible to find peace of mind that way. Take it for checking. Take a look at somebody who is powerful, who is monetarily successful. How happy are they? How satisfied are they? Do they really have peace of mind?

Let's take a look at those individuals who are trying to get happiness and peace of mind from a relationship. Does that relationship give peace of mind? Take a check and see if you have happiness with no sorrow, peace of mind, and where you are looking of it. Are you seeking it in a person who is unhappy or relatively unhappy? You must go inside yourself in order to find peace of mind and happiness. By unloading your limitations, you will discover that you are already unlimited and you can do anything you want. Just unload your limiting thoughts.

Peace of mind means a quiet mind, not a noisy mind. That is why only a few of us ever find it. We are looking for peace of mind outside ourselves and peace of mind can only be acquired by having a quiet mind. The more one quiets his or her mind, the more powerful one becomes. That is what we are going to explore.

Before sending you on to explore this rich territory with Lester, there are a few suggestions which may help you on your journey. Each of the talks you are about to read is designed to bring a key theme into your awareness. Each also represents not only thoughts for your mind to digest, but more importantly, energy for your whole being to absorb. Because of this, Lester recommends that you not hurdle your way through them. Instead, read them slowly, allowing enough time for reflection and integration. In short, approach this material as you would a private talk with a good friend. Approach it with an open heart and mind and allow it to deliver its gifts to you. Above all, by working slowly with this material you will give yourself the opportunity to practice many of the powerful and practical tools it contains. If you do this honestly and persistently, you will give yourself the opportunity to practice many of the powerful and practical tools it contains. If you do this honestly and persistently, you will give yourself a gift of inestimable value. You will discover for yourself a direct link to the source of your own wisdom. You will, as Lester so often says, "come to know that you know." And this, after all, is the ultimate goal of any true teaching.

Finally, it is important for you to know that these sessions are designed to give you a great deal more than a different intellectual perspective on the human condition. For as our guide says repeatedly in the following pages—"thinking will not get you there." Instead, this material, the questions and answers, the aphorisms, and the suggested exercises are all intended as an introduction to a remarkable, experiential process that is as simple, as clear and as powerful as the words themselves. This process is called the "Release Technique," and it is, quite simply put, a very direct, easy to use way to eliminate the boundaries of thoughts, feelings, emotions and wants which stand between you and self-realization.

So after you have spent time in these sessions, I encourage you to turn to the material in Appendix A and introduce yourself to this innovative transformation technique which Lester discovered on his journey to personal realization. Through it I believe you will discover a key to achieving the quality of life and consciousness you seek. And I know that through a loving and committed practice of it you will experience that unlimited, joyous and powerful state of being that is our natural right and our natural state.

I wish you a remarkable and joyful adventure.

Love,

Larry Crane

Larry Crane

The Power of Love

CONTENTS

PAGE

Love is Absolutely Necessary 3

Love is the Most Powerful Force in the Universe .. 9

We Never Hurt When We Love 37

Love is Acceptance 45

Love is the Answer to All Problems 79

Love is Communication 81

Love is the Cohesive Force of the Universe 87

A Love Exercise 131

Lester In His Own Words 133

A Message from Lester 145

The Power of Love

Love is Absolutely Necessary If We Ever Expect to Get Full Realization

*Lester Levenson Speaking to Students
in California, February 25, 1965*

I thought tonight I might talk on the subject of love. Love is one word I seldom use, mainly because it's so misunderstood. I also believe that through this method of growing or only through growth do we understand what love is; that by defining it we just add some more words to the usual words and it doesn't really convey the meaning of the word love. But love is an absolutely necessary ingredient on the path, if we ever expect to get full realization. We must increase our love until it is complete.

Now, the love I talk about of course has nothing to do with sex. Sex is a body gratification. However, we have confused it, most of us, very much with love. And the majority of us still tie it in with love. Although, when you see what sex is and what love is, you'll see they're two different things. They can be tied together, but they don't have to be. The love that we talk about

The Power of Love

here is the love of Jesus Christ. It's the love complete, which expressed in the extreme is "Love thy enemy."

I think the best definition of the word, as it seems to me, is love is a feelingness of givingness with no expectation of receiving for the giving. It's a very free giving. And it's an attitude that is constant. Love doesn't vary, at least the type of love we're talking about. The amount we have, we apply to everyone. We love our family as much as we love strangers. This might sound odd but this is the truth. To the degree we're capable of loving strangers, to that degree we're capable of loving our families.

The concept of possession is just the opposite of the meaning of love. In love there is never a holding on to, a fencing in, or anything like that. Love has a sense of freeing the ones we love. When we are giving, we have an attitude, we want the other one to have what the other one wants. I guess the best example of this type of love is the love of a mother for a child and sometimes a father. A mother will sacrifice and give everything to the child without considering herself.

The Power of Love

There are many other definitions for love, I'm just trying to think what they are. I think acceptance is a good word. When we love people, we accept them the way they are. If we love this world, we accept the world the way it is. We don't try to change it, we let it be. We grant the world its beingness, the same way we should grant every other person his or her beingness. Let them be the way they want to be. Never try to change them. Try to change them is injecting our own ego. We want them to be the way we would like them to be. So love is a feeling, first of all, of oneness with, of identity with the other one or all other ones. When there's a full love you feel yourself as the other person. Treating the other person is just like treating your very own self. There's complete identity.

Love is not only a feeling, love is a tremendous power which is so little understood in the world today. We have an example of this type of love being expressed today by Martin Luther King. No matter how much he's attacked, he will give out nothing but love to his attacker. He teaches non-violence. Now, the biggest demonstration of this type of love was Mahatma Gandhi's winning a war against Britain

The Power of Love

without any arms. Through teaching, the British are our brothers, we love the British, non-resistance to the British and to the British soldiers, only love for them. Gandhi understood this and was able to win over enough followers in India to make this effective.

Love is the Most Powerful Force in the Universe

The power behind love without question is far more powerful than the hydrogen bomb, once you see what love is. Love is the most powerful force in the universe. When we express love, as love is, not as we have been taught to think what love is. It is said sometimes that God is love and I say one with God is a majority. One individual with nothing but love can stand up against the entire world because this love is so powerful. Which I think leads us somewhat into seeing that this love is nothing but the self with a capital "S," that we speak of. This love is God. God is love. God is all powerful. So there's some authority for what I'm saying besides my saying it. Love will give not only all the power in the universe, it will give all the joy and all the knowledge.

The Power of Love

Now, how to make this practical? The best way of increasing our capacity to love is through wisdom, understanding. However, we can do things in our everyday life that will raise our level of love. The first place to practice love is at home with the family. We should try to love our family more and more and more. I think everyone knows the wonderful experience of love, of loving one person. So, you could imagine what it's like if you love 3 billion people. It would be 3 billion times more enjoyable.

So, home is the first place to keep trying to increase our love for the ones around us, by granting them their beingness. That's the most difficult thing, I believe, to do in a family, to grant the other one the other one's beingness, especially if the other one is a child. But every child is a whole, complete, infinite individual. Next, after loving the ones in our home, we should try to love our neighbors. Then our larger group—our state, our country. Then, we should try to love all people, all over the world.

"Even Russians?" a man asks.

Even Russians. I heard Oral Roberts say something on that some Sundays ago. He said people ask what would Jesus be like if he came back today. And he said he wouldn't be the way people expect. He wouldn't have anything against anyone. He would not hate the Communists. He would talk against doing wrong, doing evil, but he would never say anything against any human being. I believe that if we understood the power of love, in that if the majority of Americans loved the Russians, Russia would be conquered by the Americans without any arms.

And after we learn to love all the people in this world, there are many more people outside of this world. I think loving all the people in this world would allow us to meet with our brothers and sisters of other worlds because in this universe, there are many, many dimensions, many, many places of abode. And because of our incapacity to love on this planet, we have cut them off.

So, to come back to a point of being practical, the more we practice love, the more we love and the more we love, the more we can practice love. The more we

develop love, the more we come in touch with the harmony of the universe, the more delightful our life becomes, the more bountiful, the more everything. It starts a cycle going, where you spin upwards, this loving and receiving. That's another thing, if we want to be loved the way to do it is to love. It's not only the very best method, but I think it's the only method of receiving love, is to love because what we give out must come back. But looking for love without loving does not bring love to us, does not satisfy us. The happy one is the one loving, the one giving. Blessed is the giver because he's so much happier, if he gives from his heart. Are there any questions on this concept of love?

"You made a statement if you don't love someone more, you hate the other person less." says a man.

I think before that though, I'd like to remind you of another point. When we say we love one person more than another, if we would trace it through by going inwardly, we will find that the one that we love more is a person whom we think we need, that has something that we would like to have and therefore, we say we

love that person more. Actually, love cannot be chopped up. If you want to test your own love, look at your enemies. This is the real test or if you don't want to go that far, look at strangers. Examine your attitude towards strangers. It should be one of well, they are me, they are my family. Every mother should be our mother. Every father should be our father. Every child should be our child. This is the attitude we achieve through understanding. This is the real sense of the word love.

"Lester, what it seems like to me you're talking about love is giving, giving of yourself and so forth. Here's the conflict I have, occasionally, is that it seems like as you give of yourself, that people tend to take more and more and eventually it seems like they can if you don't, in effect, if you don't put a stop to things, bleed you dry, emotionally, mentally, financially and they use you as a crutch...," says Paul.

Paul, I say no, that's impossible, if we feel the real love. I'm turning right back around the other way. If we have the correct attitude of love, that doesn't happen. Now, what you're saying, I hear very often.

The Power of Love

"But don't you think that people…there's something about, I don't know. The impression I get is that love is a sign to other people in a way of weakness perhaps and it seems like there's a loss of respect. I just wonder how you can give and yet keep the respect," says Paul.

The givingness is not in things, number one. The givingness is an attitude. We can always maintain an attitude of love. Now, most people who give, are not giving lovingly, they're giving because of the credit they will get for giving. Look at me I'm doing good or I get my name in the paper or something like that. You see, that type of love will get us into trouble. People will drain us on that because were looking…

"For something in return," says Paul.

We're looking to put ourselves up in the process and therefore, they'll pull us down.

"Don't you think though, it's easier to love somebody 5,000 miles away than somebody next door to you," says Paul.

The Power of Love

The easiest thing in the universe to do is to love everyone. This is what I think. This is what I've discovered. Once we learn what love is, that's the easiest thing to do. It takes effort and agony not to love. It takes tremendous effort not to love everyone. And you see the effort being expended everyday. But when we love, we're at one with them, we're at peace and everything falls into line beautifully. The main thing is to see love in the sense I'm trying to define it. Then, those things don't happen. But when we love in the sense that humanity understands the word to mean, then you're right. But I don't call that love.

"But what do you call it?" Paul asks.

Selfishness. Actually, we're doing things to help ourselves and yet in the high love, in the spiritual love, there's no self abnegation. We don't have to hurt ourselves when we love everyone and we don't. You see in love there's a thing of mutuality. That which is mutual is correct. If you love, you hold to that love and therefore people won't take advantage of you. If you're loving, you're applying the most powerful force in the universe. But it's the love of Jesus that I'm talking

The Power of Love

about. Practically speaking, if someone is trying to hurt you and you just feel love for that person, then that person continues, you'll see them hurt themselves. They continue further, to almost destroy themselves or just knock themselves out. They won't be able to oppose you anymore. But we have to practice this love that I'm speaking of, not to love as we have known it.

"To love the way you're saying, it isn't something that you say I'm going to do. I'm going to love. I'm going to apply this to and love this person so much he's going to kill himself," Paul says.

No, that wouldn't be love.

"It's a basic attitude, its nothing you're physically or even mentally doing. It's just a concept," Paul says.

It's a constant attitude that evolves in us when we try to develop it. However, we should try practicing the love, as I said before, first on our family. Grant everyone in the family their own beingness, if you can. If you can't, keep trying, keep trying until you can. Then, apply it to friends, then, strangers, then,

The Power of Love

everyone. See, by doing this you will develop it. Although, as you say, it isn't something you can turn on just like that.

"Just like beingness, you, in a way is all we do have, all of us have it. It's layered over by many attitudes," says Paul.

It's smothered by wrong attitudes. Now, this love I talk about is our basic nature, it's a natural thing, that's why it's so easy. The opposite takes effort. We move away from our natural self. Cover it, smother it with concepts of the opposite of love. Then because we're not loving, unloving comes back at us and proves to us the concepts like Paul brought out, which we all experience when we first start practicing this love. You're not alone Paul.

"Isn't love almost like a selfishness? Because when you love somebody it's such a wonderful feeling for you...," says woman.

Well, this is a matter of semantics that I don't want to get involved in. The way you put it, yes, but not in a general sense.

The Power of Love

"I know when I love somebody, I feel so good...," says woman.

It's true, after you discover what love is. It's the greatest thing in the universe. It's a thing everyone wants only because it's its basic nature, in the first place. Every human being is basically a extremely loving individual.

"Does it come down to this thing of pleasure and is it the same type of thing where your mind becomes still in one avenue of thought, of concentration, of acceptance of the other person and therefore the mind is still," says Harry.

Yes.

"The true nature then comes through, which is the love," continues Harry.

Yes. Yes. The more we love, the less we have to think. If I'm not loving you, I have to be on guard. I have to protect myself. If I'm not loving the world, I'm always protecting myself from the world, which causes more and more and more thoughts, puts me

The Power of Love

extremely on a defensive and subconsciously it builds up, year in and year out. Then, I'm a mass of thoughts, protecting myself from the world, see. Now, if I love the world, the world can't hurt me, my thoughts get quiet, the mind gets peaceful and then that infinite self is right there and that's the experience of this tremendous joy.

"In other words, it's not the object that brings this out, it's the quieting of the mind that lets us actually being come through. It really is the love experience, isn't it?" says Harry.

Yes.

"More than the object. When we say it's the object that we love...," continue Harry.

But, it's actually what you say. You're taking it right from the top now.

"The shine coming through...," says Harry.

What Harry is saying is that we take our infinite beingness, our infinite joy and we cover it over with

thoughts. We take the natural state, which is unlimited, we cover it up with thoughts of limitation. The thoughts smother this infinite self that we are. It smothers the capacity to enjoy. And so, all we need to do is to quiet the thoughts or rid ourselves of all thoughts. Now, what's left over is the infinite, glorious being that we are, which is our natural state. Isn't that odd? It's our natural state, that's the way we were, that's the way we're going to be. We are actually that now, but we don't see it. This infinite glorious being that we are, being absolutely perfect can never change. It's always there, we just don't look at it, we look away from it, we look far away from it. What we should do is turn our mind inward and begin looking at it and the more we look at it with a capital "I," the more we see It.

Everything seems to point to the same direction, doesn't it? That happens as we get more understanding of what life and the universe is. Everything fits together more and more, until it gets simpler and simpler, until it's just one absolute simple called God. God is simple, everything else is complex. The greater the complexity, the further we are from God. That's

The Power of Love

The Power of Love

why God is one and only one or one without a second. Have I covered the subject of love?

"In practice, then if someone else has a heartfelt desire and our heart, I'm going to use that word, that same feeling and there's a feeling, if I went along with him, I might lose something, than that isn't love. But if it was complete in the sense that whatever they wish, I wish because their feeling must be my feeling, is only one feeling. Then, I wouldn't be afraid. But if I'm afraid…," Bob says.

There's a word for it today called togetherness. It's a very good word. Doesn't that fit what you're saying? Togetherness, together we see one, the same thing, we want the same thing. Is that…

"Seems a little weak, in a sense, to me," continues Bob.

But that's the word being used. I think we'd be better off if we dropped the word love and used words like togetherness, oneness.

The Power of Love

"...the thought occurred to me that when you're trying to align your interest with another interest. I have the attitude that I know my beingness or I feel that I'm lined up, I can't get hurt. So therefore, how can anybody else hurt me? So therefore, I want the other person to have what they want also because, again, this mutuality thing. I know that I can't get hurt, so I know I must extend the same privilege. It isn't a thing that I have to line up mutually here or, you know, same ideas or align myself with anybody. I just know that I'm on the track, that I'm alright. Then everything else, then nothing can hurt me, regardless of what other attitudes there are," Paul says.

That's true.

"So then you just accept you love or you accept all situations for everybody because it has to be good for them it can't only be good for you regardless of others..." Paul continues.

We Never Hurt When We Love

It's impossible to be hurt when we love fully. We are never hurt when we love fully. We are never hurt when we love. We only feel wonderful when we love. In fact, we feel the greatest when we love.

"Excuse me. If we have a feeling differentiating, though more of course in the beginning, when you say practice in your home. But if you don't feel a sense of togetherness with one more than another, then you begin to separate one's self," Bob says.

It's not full love, it's partial love. And the more partial it is, the less good it feels. When we love all the time, we love every being, we have nothing but tremendously wonderful, warm attitude of everything is fine, every person is just right. We wear our rose colored glasses. That's the way we see the world when we love. When we hate, we see the same world, in just the opposite way. So it's a tremendous thing to learn this little secret of the power of love.

The Power of Love

I just wonder if I shouldn't read off some of the definitions in *The Ultimate Truth* book (*The Ultimate Truth About Love & Happiness* by Lester Levenson), there's so many ways its been said.

I got these five pages on it. I remember before this book came out I said I never know what to say on love, there isn't much you can say about it. But I did and this was gathered over many, many talks. I could see it's an attempt to convey the concept of the real love by saying it in as many ways as possible. Well, the first one, "Love is a feeling of givingness, with no thought of receiving any return for it." That's the one I started with. "Love is giving with no strings attached."

"Only by loving does love come to us." The more we love, the more love comes to us. I know this is a basic error in many, many people's thinking. They go through life wanting to be loved, never feeling that they are, even when they are really getting the love. Because the feeling has to be in us. If I love you, I feel wonderful. If you love me, you feel wonderful. As you said before, it's the one who loves who feels great. So,

wanting to be loved is getting into a direction that can never be satisfied.

"Don't you then give the love that you get back?" Bob asks. "You have to be the love that you feel."

"In loving you feel wonderful," woman says.

"But you seem to have an objective to love but you're really feeling your own love that you're giving to the other person," Bob continues.

You see its different concepts of the word love in different people. It might not just suit your concept what Bob says, but I know what Bob means and I say yes. But you'll always be right because you think that way and thinking makes it so. Love is an attitude, a feeling and requires no action, Paul. It might have action. You might give away everything you have, but it's not necessarily so that you should or would give away everything. The main thing is the attitude.

"Does a child love?," Paul asks.

A child loves a little more than we do, but not too much more. Because a child comes into the world with attitudes developed over the millenniums. A child is not a new thing at birth, it's a sum total of the entire past. But since the child just hasn't met with the world, the cruel, cruel world, yet, a child has not taken on more concepts of the opposite of love and in that sense a child loves more than an adult, everything else being equal. The main thing that a child wants from us is love and we cannot fool a child. They know our feelings and that's what they feel. They don't listen to the words that we put out. We fool ourselves with the words, but we don't fool the children. But giving love to a child will develop love in that child this lifetime, will condition the child for a very or a most happy life. But before we can love a child we have to know what love is, develop it and be capable of loving. That's why I've always said to mothers, you want to help your children, help yourself. That's the very best way of helping your children. Right, Dawn.

Looking for our lies now. And you'll notice that the children understand it immediately and reciprocate. The reason why we have a hassle with children today,

The Power of Love

is mainly because we don't know what love is. If we were capable of loving, instead of the conflict with children, it would be just the opposite, it would be a complete harmony between parent and child. It's only because we have lost sight of what love is, that we are in this difficulty of opposition between parent and child. There's hardly a family in which this does not exist today, it's just a matter of how little it is. Because the world, as it is today, is in a very confused state knows very little of the real values that we came here for and is lost in chasing, the god money, prestige and so forth.

Love is Acceptance

Love is acceptance. Love is taking people as they are. Love is loving the other one because the other one is the way the other one is. Love is trust. When we love people, we will always trust them. You can use these things as a check upon yourself. If you don't trust someone, you don't love them. That's not an easy one to see and I suggest you work that out yourself. If you don't trust someone, you don't love them. I say, trust the most crooked person in the world and that person

The Power of Love

will be honest with you. Love is a feelingness of peace. As we said before, when we love we have no enemies, we don't have to be on guard and we're at ease. Love is identification. It is being the other one by identifying with the other one. Love is what every being is seeking through his every act. That's a powerful one.

Love is identification. It is being the other one by identifying with the other one. You feel as though the other one is you. You identify with them.

"What I was saying before though, if I realize my beingness and only good can come to me, that I'm in the spirit of this love and so on. Then why is it necessary to identify with anybody?" Paul asks.

If you're in that spirit, then you automatically identify with everyone. It goes together.

"You're thinking about two levels, you're thinking the spiritual and are we talking mainly here about physical bodies?" Paul asks.

When I say identify, you are me. When I know that, that's identification complete. I also know your every

The Power of Love

thought and feeling, if you are me. That's how complete the identification becomes. This actually happens.

"It becomes, I am my father_____, I am my brother_____, I am my sister_____" a man says.

"Put in practice, if Paul and I are after the same piece of real estate, for example, and we're bidding against each other, my thought would have to be or my feeling would have to be, it doesn't really matter who gets it," Bob says.

Yes, Paul should have it.

"We both have it," Bob says. "See what happens. Pardon?"

"If you say Paul should have it…" woman says.

"It's a mutual, one-hearted feeling. If I cannot feel loss if he gets it and he could not feel loss if I got it," Bob says.

You should enjoy his getting it.

The Power of Love

"True, or he would enjoy my getting it," Bob says.

Right.

"So, it wouldn't matter anymore than if two people who, in a sense of young lovers wanted something, they'd both want it, it would almost be the same sensation. If the other one gets it, then joy! Isn't that true? Whatever we do, with whom ever we are or even if our enemy gets it, it should have that joy. But who's our enemy then?" Bob asks.

It's a very good question. If you love your enemy you have no more enemies.

"Well, I've made it a practice now, that when any of my friends or acquaintances.

I know or anybody else comes and tells me about a terrific deal they've made, I always grab for their hand and shake it and tell them how happy I am regardless of where it was or if it was something I was trying to buy for a client or anything else, I always tell them that, and believe me the surprised looks that I get show me the success that I've had with a lot of these

people. They're telling me for one reason but I feel real joy at their happiness and good fortune because I feel I'm gaining something too," a man says.

The power and effect of love is obvious, just try it, apply it, like you're doing on that, on other things. The effect is obvious, it's a very powerful thing.

"You know I think that point is really good at accepting people as they are and not by any virtue or anything it's just always been fairly easy for me to do. So I don't know, I just figure its part of me and don't work to attain it, I guess the question I have or I'm more skeptical. What happens when these people have an effect on your life that to your way of thinking, your concept affects you adversely. Isn't there room here for constructive criticism or pointing out the truth as you see it and still accepting them as they are? This is something I, just the last few weeks have done a great deal of thinking about, for one reason or another, is I think in the past as I've accepted people for what they are and said, well as a human being if I was raised like he was and taught like he did, I'd do exactly the same thing, but what happens, it seems like, anyhow, is that

I guess I would say I tolerate them, perhaps more than accept them," Paul says.

Right.

"But I can't appreciate them when they do something that affects me in an adverse manner," Paul continues.

Paul, we shouldn't look upon them as human beings subject to error. If you saw the absolute truth you'd see infinite, perfect beings. Now, I say this is the truth. Everyone is an infinite perfect being. That when we see them otherwise, we're not seeing the truth. So you see what it does to your concept. I say you're looking at them wrongly and you'll be hurt because of that.

"But what happens if you see them as a perfect being and perfect in their own right, and so forth, and yet something happens that by appearances, anyhow…," Paul says.

By appearances, yeah.

"Looks like its affecting you or your family adversely. Then, what do you have to say then? I'm just not seeing right, huh?" Paul asks.

Change your view. Change your thought. Change something in you and it'll change out there immediately.

"Change your thought," Paul says.

If you don't like the world out there, you must change yourself and immediately the world rightens. Gets to where we want it to be.

"Well, doesn't this mean though, that if you carry this attitude, right on through, not just to this person, but to this country or the whole world and so forth, this world would never change? In other words, isn't all the so called progress brought about by dissatisfaction with people or situations as they exist?" asks Paul.

No, just the opposite. Dissatisfaction throws a monkey wrench into the works. When there's love, progress is the very greatest. I just read one here that love is what every being is seeking through his every

act. If you will trace through all your behavior or the behavior of people, what are they looking for? They're looking for love. That's the ultimate. That is the greatest of all progress, is love. Our life is getting far too complex and it's not progress because people are not happier today. I think that's the proof, their happiness. They have thing like they've never had it before. Look at the mess we're in today or don't you see it?

"No, well, I guess it really depends on how you look at it. No, I don't think, I think, I guess that's where I have to differ, I think things are better than ever, I mean the world as a whole. I guess because I think that there is less pain the world today, from a medical stand point, we'll say. There's probably more, I suppose, mental pain," Paul says.

The greatest pain is mental, there's more anxiety and dissatisfaction today than there ever was in our time.

"But, I think, just in my own thinking, I'm not the expert here, but I just think that's because of an

unwillingness to adjust, to accept, you might say," Paul says.

I say it's a lack of love. Well, I could put it another way. It's not that we have less love today as much as it is we were so busy, busily occupied in trying to make a living, we didn't have time to be with ourselves. Now, we have time to be with ourselves. Thirty years ago we thought, oh, if we only had things we would be happy and we were striving very hard to get things. Now, we've gotten the things, instead of being happy, we find ourselves less happy, which is good because our next big lesson is to learn that happiness is not in things. It'll go more toward principle in the near future. But we're coming down now to a dangerously, to a dangerous point of getting away from the absolute truth by accepting some of the things of the world as they really shouldn't be accepted by us. We should see the perfection where the seeming imperfection seems to be because we are aiming for the very top. I know I'm not satisfying you very much, Paul. Am I?

"Well, I'm one of these persons that when I hear something I don't form anything, I just kind of let time to sink in...," Paul says.

It's something I can't give you. I can make words and you have to do something with them and if you see what I see, then you'll see it. If you don't, well, work with it, maybe someday you will. But you got a good base to work from, as you said before, it was easy for your to accept people as they are.

The Power of Love

"The person then seems to want something, it would really be perfectly alright with me to go along knowing that all is perfect and it doesn't matter to me what they want. It's possible for me to give it to them. It would be, I being them knowing there's only perfection doesn't matter if there's only perfection that comes from it. But if I'm afraid then, I'm separating myself from seeing something besides God, something besides perfection," says Bob.

Now, one of the keys to abundance is the spirit of giving. The key to supply is to develop a constant feeling of givingness. This is a real key in producing supply. If we had an attitude of givingness every moment, and we want the things, they would smother us. A constant attitude of gratitude is also a very helpful thing.

"That's love?" a man asks.

"Gratitude is something that doesn't make sense to me," says Bob.

Then drop it. There's a lot of other words here that could make sense. See, all these things I say, to me, are

all the same things. Almost everything I say is the same thing again and again, in different words, in different phrases. I smiled before when Harry saw how this thing of love was the same as something else. In the end, it all comes down to one thing, and only one. So stick to the words that you like and let go of the words you don't.

"Because, after all, it's only your own concept of any word that brings you a realization of the meaning of that word. You mean you have your own concept of it,"a man says.

To me, all these words mean the same thing. Love is acceptance, identification, understanding, communication, truth, God, you, me, it's all the same thing and it will be to everyone if they'll look at it to the same, from the same point, from your very own center. If you look at it from your very own center, you'll see that it's all the same. Your very own center, being your very own self with a capital "S," the real you that you are. Not this fake ego that we're trying to make a big thing of.

"All our schooling, all education, everything is, and has been, given to us and now we're trying to bring it all together," says Harry

That's why I've said education is actually a system of learned ignorance, it's a miseducation, as it is today. All the important things in life are never taught. No matter how many years you go to college you don't get any courses on happiness, love, life; all these subjects that are so important, that everyone is seeking, there's not a single course in any college in this country on it.

"Everybody'd paid 'cause it's a snap course," says Harry.

"We don't have any properly qualified teachers. The game must be played," a man says.

"We have one that's pretty close," a man says.

It's an attitude of givingness, it's not an actual givingness of things. Now, giving things could be part of it. And giving things could be just the opposite of love. I can give you things because I want you to like

me, that's not love on my part, that's trying to bolster my ego.

"You're seeking love," a man says.

However, the greatest givingness that can be given is to give understanding, to give wisdom. If a man asks me for a meal and I give it to him, five hours later he needs it again. But if I get across to him the principle on how to produce a meal, he'll never go hungry again. So, the greatest givingness is understanding, wisdom.

"I was going to say before, when Paul was talking about the other person doing things which may seem to be against you to gain his end, but really he's merely attempting to gain love by doing this for someone in his field. And therefore, if you understand that understanding and you know he's doing it to gain love or for love, that's seeing through this misconception of the person," a man says.

Carry that through to the extreme and you'll see every person, in his every act, is seeking love.

"Alright. Then, if I know that and it seems though he's doing something against me, I know he's doing something for him and therefore he can't be doing it against me. I know that," a man says.

And as long as you know it, you are correct. Nothing can be done against you.

"Well, it's just that circle, if he's doing it for himself, then he's doing it for you, too. Right Kenny?" a man says.

"Yeah. Micro to macro," Kenny responds.

"Micro to macro. That's right." man agrees.

"But if a person hesitates to give things it's because he feels he doesn't have it all and that he would be taking something from himself," Bob says.

It's in the attitude, not in the actual giving or not giving.

"But if you see so many people who are frightened when they speak of giving things and I don't see the

The Power of Love

difference. If they are so capable mentally, certainly they have all the things they need to give," Bob says.

"Sometimes giving sustains the basic thought behind the condition bringing about the giving," Harry says.

"Wow," man says.

"Like you are investing in a heart fund, say, if I feel love to the heart disease, then I give to the heart's fund, so to speak. Right? If I would want to actually fight heart disease, I would see the imperfection in the thought, in the thing and know the perfection," Harry says.

There's all levels of helping, all degrees of helping.

"So, a lot of this giving to charities and some other things is really a sustaining of the condition of which we think we're giving to eliminate," Harry says.

Mmm, hmm.

The Power of Love

"Keeping it in mind, therefore sustaining it. And again, of course, the bigger thing behind it all is you say…," Harry says.

"The perfection," man says.

"Well, yes, perfection, but the attitude on our part of the spiritual giving, of the lifting, of not sustaining the condition, but of lifting spiritually above the condition, so that you don't, so that you see the perfection" Harry says.

"Seeing the perfection, instead of the imperfection," man says.

"Yeah," Harry agrees.

When you do that, you will affect every atom in this universe. You will affect every person, whether they realize it or not because you're invoking a power that's most powerful. It's loving every person into a perfect being, minus all these negativities of diseases. And you actually do far more for all the heart disease with that attitude, than you would by giving money. But, I'm trying to make a point that it's not important whether

you give money to them or not. The important thing is your attitude. You can give for the glory of giving or being put up as a giver. That does you no good. Or you could have the attitude of what you just said and actually give no cash and you're doing far more good. So, it's the attitude that's important.

Love is the Answer to All Problems

Love is the answer to all problems. No matter what the problem is, if you will just apply love to the fullest extent possible and succeed, that problem will drop away immediately. Just don't get aggravated. Just know that everything is fine, everything is alright and just feel love and you'll see that problem resolve itself, no matter how difficult a problem it is. When there are problems, if we would love more they would disappear. When the love is complete, the problem dissolves immediately.

The Power of Love

Love is Communication

Love is communication. Communication and love go together. Communication is getting across an idea. I say "Frank tarrarrarrarra" and you say "Oh yeah, tarrarrarrarra." See, it's an idea from me to Frank and acknowledgement of it. That's communication. We both see eye to eye on the same thing. Now,....

"Now this is very important, lets stop right there for a minute. What did you just say? We both see eye to eye. Alright. Now, let's forget about this eye. Right?" man asks.

Yeah.

"Okay," man says.

Well, that I to I meant, it's an expression. I didn't mean a physical eye.

"Alright. Okay. So that these people understand," man replies.

I, I.

The Power of Love

"That's good," man says.

"See, see," Bob says.

"I, I," man repeats.

You can easily test this out on your own life. That if you increase communication with an individual you increase the love between the two of you. Just practicing communication. Say something to them, have them acknowledge that they got it by repeating it and go on and on that way and the love between the two of you will keep going up and up. Increasing communication, increases love and the other way around—increasing love, increases communication. You'll notice, the more you love, the more you're able to communicate with people. Can I add something, Bob? It's a very interesting thing that can be tested very easily, just increase communication and you'll see love. Do it with someone who's against you.

"You betcha, because, you know why? Because as Paul said before, if someone appears to be doing something that appears to be against you, there is a lack of communication between I and I. And if you do,

if you open up that channel of communication and you see eye to eye and there is no wrong or anything that this man is doing that is foreign to you because your awareness of him is raised to such a degree that there is perfect understanding between the I and I. Isn't that right, Ted?" man asks.

"I can't see if Lester shook his head or not," Ted responds.

Another thing happens as love increases, reality in the world increases also. The more we're capable of loving, the more we'll see things exactly the way they happen. Now, if you practice increasing your reality in the world, your love will go up, too. Just in the same way if you practice increasing communication, your love will go up. Or the converse, the more we love, the more we see things the way they are, in the world. If we were all very loving people, every time there'd be an accident, we'd all see it alike.

"You probably wouldn't see the accident," Harry says.

That's further up, Harry. If you have the love complete, there never would be an accident.

"Because we wouldn't have concepts of accidents," Harry says.

Here it is. Love is communing. Love is communication. Lending support, wanting for the other one, what the other one wants, that is love. The greatest help or giving one may give to another is to help the other to get the understanding of truth. In this way, one gives the other the formula for happiness.

Love is the Cohesive Force of the Universe

Love is the cohesive force of the universe. Love is attracting, integrating and constructive; and so affects everything and anything it's applied to. Parliaments cannot right the world, but enough individuals feeling love, can. I think that's an interesting point for our present times. You cannot legislate a correct world. Parliaments will never straighten this world out. Only when the individuals, the majority of people in this

world have an attitude of love will the world be a nice place to live in, will it be harmonious.

Almost all people mistake ego approval for love. Because it is not love, it is not satisfying. Consequently, one continuously needs and demands it. And this produces only frustration.

Boy, the next one is a hard one. I'm just going to read it and skip over it. Love is not an emotion. Or maybe I shouldn't skip over it. When I say love is not an emotion, emotion is energy in motion, it's an intense, active, disturbing thing, an emotion is. The emotion of love is the most peaceful of feeling. And in that sense, I mean love is not an emotion.

People need each other and think it is love. There's no hanging on to or fencing in of the other one, when one loves. Human love does not want to share its love with others, but rather wants its own personal satisfaction. Real love wants to share its love and the more it is shared the more joyous it is. There is no longing for in love because longing is separation. Love being oneness it does not allow separation. True love

cannot be gotten through marriage, it must be there before marriage or developed during marriage.

It is Impossible to Love One and Hate Another

Love cannot be applied to one and not to another. It is impossible to love one and hate another. When we love one more than another, that one is doing something for us, that is human love. When one loves people because they are nice to him, that too is human love. True love is unconditional. In true love one loves even those who oppose him. See, the next sentence is a real test of where we stand on the subject love. We should love everyone equally. This is a tremendous yard stick for checking yourself on growth. Equal mindedness towards all beings, loving everyone equally, is actually the top state.

"Isn't the secret of love really a realization that you have all and he has all; therefore, there's no separation," Bob says.

Yes.

"Because if you say he's got something I haven't got, that's where difficulty comes in. It's like sitting on a pile of sand. You have a pile of sand, I have a pile of sand. I put a little mark on it and you say 'I want your river.' And I say 'Well, you got a pile of sand and you just have to make a mark on it and you have the river.' And you say 'I want your river.' But it's nothing but a pile of sand, it's just a word, river. I have all and you have all, so there's no fuss, is there?" asks Bob.

That's right. When you see the truth, everyone has exactly the same amount, it's infinite.

"So if you want what I've got it's simply because you don't see you're already sitting on a pile of sand and you can have the sand, too, because you're sitting on it," Bob says.

Mmm hmm. It's that simple.

"So I say you've got the sand. You say you want mine. Well, you can have mine 'cause it's infinite sand. I don't care. So, if I say, 'I can't have,' well that's the difficult. I say, 'Well I'm not sitting on infinite sand,'" Bob says.

The Power of Love

It's making an untrue. It's making a lie out of the truth.

"So love is really pointing out, well you're sitting on a pile of sand, like I'm sitting on a pile of sand. Take the sand. And this is all the thoughts we get in through our thinking," Bob says.

Right.

"But we say, 'No we don't,' we say, 'I have something and you don't have something.' Isn't that all the cause of our difficulty?" Bob asks.

It's awakening to the fact that we have everything.

"And this comes first, doesn't it, before love?" Bob asks.

We can work at it from both sides.

"Well, I can't love something, if Harry's got something that I haven't got; how can I love Harry if I want it? It's only if I have it and he has it and if he has it, he can't take anything from me. So, we both love

each other because we both have it. We don't fight over the air," Bob says.

"But if you say to Harry, 'Harry I love you because you've got something there that belongs to one of us,'" man says.

"I love you because," a woman chimes in.

"Isn't that right?" man asks.

"Because together we admire and feel good towards that same infinite capacity that have. Isn't that right?" Bob asks.

Mmm, hmm.

"There's no separation in our capacity to have," Bob continues.

"You're imperative is the same as my imperative. So what's the fight?" Harry says.

"There's none," Bob says.

"None," Harry agrees.

The Power of Love

"So all we can do is enjoy the same thing. There's nothing but enjoyment," Bob affirms.

"That's what Lester said," a woman says.

"Whether they're morons or professors. We all have the same," Harry says.

"That's right," man agrees.

"It's concepts that's made it otherwise," Harry says.

"That's right," man concurs.

"I think that Harry's doing meditation on his own," man says.

When the revelations start coming, they come. Just don't stop them. Let them keep coming.

"You're sitting there and all of the sudden, you put your finger to your head like this and you say, 'POW, I got something there,'" man says.

It's been there all the time though, that's the odd part of it.

"It's just realizing it," man says.

All we do is open our eyes to something that's been there all the time.

"But it's usually something exactly different than what you thought it was," man says.

Yeah, the concept was wrong.

"Yes," man says.

And you let go of the wrong concept, and there it is.

"Sure. That's why you say the truth was right behind the thought," man says.

"That just became simple," man says.

Stop the thought, stop all thinking and...

"The truth is right behind the limitation," Harry finishes.

One Should Strive to Love, Never to Be Loved

It is impossible to get love. Only by loving can one feel love. The more one looks for love, the more one doesn't love. It's kind of indicting. One should strive to love, never to be loved. To be loved brings temporary happiness, ego inflation. When one loves fully, one can have no concept of not being loved. When one loves fully, one can have no concept of not being loved. I think that's a good one.

"It comes back to this thing of beingness, doesn't it? We know if we experience our beingness we can't feel any desire or we don't care what the other guy thinks, really. I mean, you know, physically speaking because…" Harry says.

That's it!

"Your it. I am what I am," Harry continues.

When love is felt for the enemy, it makes the enemy impotent, powerless to hurt us. If the enemy persists in trying to hurt us, he will only hurt himself.

One does not increase his love, one merely gets rid of one's hate. That's what you brought up before,

right? We can't increase our love because that's our natural state. Behind these concepts of non-love is always the infinite love that we are. You can't increase it. All you can do is peel away these concepts of hatred, so that this tremendous loving being that we are is not hidden. Actually, we don't keep increasing our love, we just keep doing away with the limited concepts of hate that we've had before. And by hate, I mean anything that's not love—fear, envy, jealousy, apathy, all those attitudes are different degrees of hate, at least the way I use it they are. And so we really don't increase our love, we undo our attitudes of hate.

"What are our sins, then?" Harry asks.

Our attitudes of hate. Our thoughts of limitation. The greatest sin of all sins, the downfall, is the ego sense— I am an individual separate from the all. That's the real fall into mankind.

"This is what Jesus was meaning when he mentioned sins. It wasn't the prostitutes..." Harry says.

The Power of Love

Oh, no. Everything we do prostitutes God, practically, not only prostitution, almost everything does.

"But just to show you how little sins are or the meaningless of sins, spell it backwards, pronounce it backwards. What does it mean? Nothing. Really. Snis Whoever heard of snis? What does it mean?" man asks.

It sounds like nice, backwards.

You know, evil spelled backwards is live. So you got to be careful with that backwards stuff.

"Is someone tickling you over there?" Tim asks.

"Well, she's feeling my love, Tim," Frank responds.

"She's feeling herself. Only you can feel your love." Tim says.

"You have it your way. I'll have it my way," Frank says.

"That's his concept," man says.

The Power of Love

"You know, while you were mentioning that they don't have any courses on joy or happiness or peace that are taught in colleges. Well, I thought the one that comes across is sex education," man says.

"I think you're being precocious again," man says.

"You have it your way...," man says.

"I think you have a point there," man says.

"I think Will Rogers had the same feeling. I read his biography. And in his biography he made a statement, 'I have never met a man or a person I couldn't learn to love,'" man says.

Yeah. There's another way of saying it, that he never met a stranger. But that is the concept and that was his feeling about people it shows in his philosophies and his humor. He had love.

"That's why he left this circle. He was needed somewhere else very quickly," man says.

Don't you think he was needed here?

"Well, we could use him right now," man responds.

"I remember seeing him on a stage with that rope…," man says.

"My interpretation of the word stranger is a friend that I don't know his name," man says.

"That's perfect," a man says.

I think the word name used to mean nature. Name and nature were the same word. 'Cause people were named by the nature of their work. Right? I lost the point I was going to bring out, after what you said. What did you say?

"A stranger is a friend whose name I do not know," man repeats.

Oh, whose nature I do not know, is what I wanted to imply. His nature is my beingness. He is me. Sounds like bad English, doesn't it? He is me.

"This is the top realization, though, that you're speaking of now, right?" Harry asks.

The Power of Love

Someday you'll look around and you'll just see yourself everywhere you look. You'll have a feeling, you are me, without a question. Without a doubt, you are me.

"Putting the pieces together, but I haven't yet," Harry says.

You could. That word I is the exact same I, no matter who uses it.

"Soon as we all see I to I a little more," a man says.

"How do you spell that? E-y-e?" man asks.

"I. Capital I," the man responds.

When you get to top state, you have a consciousness. There's a constant I, I, I, goes on, on the top state. That's all you see, hear, feel, think, know, just I, I, I, which is your beingness. As beingness that never changes. Beingness always is.

"Is becoming the opposite of being? Well, don't you have to become before you be?" Paul asks.

The Power of Love

"You have to be before you become," man says.

No. The becoming is an apparency. You are. I am that I am. It's an amness.

"I don't know. I guess the way I visualize it is you're you. You know, you're being, but before you can be you have to take off these coats or jackets or whatever they are. I think of them as coats in your becoming…" Paul says.

Blinders. Blinders.

"Well, alright, blinders. But isn't that the becoming?" Paul asks.

It's the apparent becoming, yes. But you are, so how can you become? It's only an apparency that you are becoming.

"It seems like to me, you are not there yet, so you have to, ah…" Paul says.

It seems that way. You're right. So therefore it seems as though you are becoming. But that's a seemingness.

The Power of Love

That's not the truth. The truth is you are, here and now.

"You're omnipresent," man says.

"Right now, you're home spanking the kids," man says.

"Well, I guess I could see that. But I mean it's, to me, what you're saying, I can't quite understand it, I guess…," Paul says.

"I'm in West Covina. I just haven't got there, yet," Paul says.

No. You are there now, but you got the silly limited concept that you're only here. That you're only that body and only through that body can you be somewhere. That's not true. If you would see the truth, you'd see everything going on at home, right now, as you're talking with me.

"You probably can, right now," man says.

er of Love

"You better believe I hear the turmoil right now…," man says.

"Proves to us that he is omnipresent, 'cause we see him here, don't we? But he can be back there anytime he wants to," a man says.

"So, he is there, really," a man says

"So, gives us something to talk about at lunch break," a man says.

But these are things we can't talk ourselves into. These are things we have to realize on our own. We have to see it through our own minds eye, so to speak. Otherwise it's just words. Someone who doesn't think he's omnipresent says, 'That's ridiculous, I'm right here.' So, until we realize this, it has no meaning, really, for us. But I say try to realize it and boy what meaning it'll take on when you find you are, always have been, always will be omnipresent.

"Watch who you tell this to though, Paul. They'll put you down at the happy pond," a man warns.

The Power of Love

"I guess, I don't particularly care what other people think of me or my feelings. I like them for what they are. If they don't like me for what they are, that's their problem," Paul says.

It's a good chance, it's a good opportunity to grow when people are saying things about you, opposing you. It gives you a chance to practice the real love. It gives you a chance to practice the real peace. Because they're making sounds with their mouth is no reason why you should feel bad about it. Opposition is a very healthy thing if it provokes growth.

So love is a thing the world sings about, writes about, has moving pictures about...

"But knows little about," the man finishes.

And knows very little about. Love is portrayed in the movies as always a male and a female winning each other. The real love is winning the universe, not just one person, but every individual in the universe.

"How about Bob?" a man asks.

The Power of Love

"He's an ardent lover," a man says.

"Well, I wouldn't go that far," a man says.

"It's in your level now," Paul says.

"Well this is a mixed group," a man says.

In the practical end of it, I left out: Square all with love. This is an excellent gimmick. During the day, if we try to fit everything into love, whatever we're doing, it will make for rapid and tremendous progress. Square all with love—am I doing this with love?—no matter what it is, try to do it with love.

"There's also another sentence there," a man says.

What?

"Assume responsibility for all your own being," a man replies.

That's another gimmick. Both of those are excellent for daily growth. Take full responsibility for whatever happens to you, no matter what it is say, what did I do to cause this? You'll develop the habit of bringing up

the cause for what's happening to you. You'll prove to yourself that you are the master, that you caused everything. And since you are the master you can uncause or cause what you would like to have caused. But taking full responsibility and squaring all with love are two excellent means of growth that can be used everyday in our relationships with people.

"Let's have a little clear communication here, Frank. Just what is your meaning?" a man asks.

"You see how that communication bit really is important," a man says.

"For who?" Frank asks.

"Everybody," a man answers.

"I don't care if anyone understands what you're talking about," Frank says.

"Well that's your opinion. I mean, that's your concept," a man says.

"We're having fun," Frank says.

The Power of Love

"There's three of us in this room instead of just one," a man says.

"I, I, I," Frank says.

"I was wondering, in your own experience, when did you, what were the steps, what breakthrough did you get as you were leading up to seeing all, yourself as all?" Harry asks.

"You feel through an open elevator shaft when you did," a man says.

That wouldn't help you anyway. What will help you is for you to do it, take those steps.

"There ain't no shortcut, Harry," Frank says.

"The first inkling I had…," a man says.

There is a shortcut.

"There is?" Frank asks.

Knowing who you are. How long does it take an omnipotent, omniscient being to know he is

The Power of Love

omnipresent and omniscient? He's got all power, all knowledge. Now, how long should it take him to realize that he has it, if he's got it? Could be done in a second.

A Love Exercise

Look at people around you and say, "I am you." Look at one person at a time and watch what happens. Do this silently.

LESTER IN HIS OWN WORDS

Thank you, Greetings and Love to each and every one of you. I think the biggest surprise tonight was to me. I didn't know I was going to talk until about 10 minutes before eight this evening, when I was told I was going to be the surprise.

So I began thinking, "What am I going to talk about? Talk about you, talk about me?" Then I realized, "What's the difference? We are all in the very same boat called life." We're all doing, in my eyes, the exact same thing that I did. We are all looking for the summum bonum. The highest good in the ultimate place. It is happiness, and we are without it all the time. Struggling for it, looking for it, wondering where it is?

Back in 1952, I claimed I found the place. It is right where I am. It is right where you are, and all this looking for it everywhere, every day year in and year out, is such a waste of time—when it is right where you are. We're all here in this classroom called earth, trying to discover something, the ultimate. And we are

all looking for it externally where it isn't. If we would only turn our direction back upon ourselves, we would discover it right here, right where I am, right where you are, right in your very own being.

I say are you, you say yes. I say that's it. Do nothing else but that, and you will be in the ultimate state of happiness. So why don't you do it? You are so habituated in looking for it over there, over there in him, in her, in this job—and it is never there. So we are all going through the same trip of trying to discover what is this all about, where is my happiness, and when we stop chasing after it out there and we turn inward, we discover that all these hard negative, terrible feelings are only a feeling. And that it is possible to get rid of these feelings by releasing them. All these feelings are subconscious programs—every bit of them put in as prosurvival—it's not only fear, but survival. All our feelings have been programmed in to automatically keep us surviving. They keep looking out there, trying to survive, keeping our minds active subconsciously 24 hours a day, so never do we stop to think and discover what we are. If you could stop your thinking for one moment, you would go through the

most tremendous experience that there is. That you are the totality of this universe in your beingness, that when your mind goes quiet, you will automatically see that—I am the most terrific being in this universe. I am whole, complete, and perfect. I always was, I am now and I always be.

So what is it that is keeping us from being in the most delectable state that there is? Simply the accumulated programs called feelings. All these negative feelings have us constantly struggling to survive, having us constantly struggling to survive, having us constantly looking away from this tremendous thing that we are, and all we need to do is quiet that mind and become self-obvious to ourselves of this tremendous being that we are.

How do we do it? I say it's simple. The Release® Technique. It happens to be the fastest, the most effective way there is to achieve this high state of being. When we are in total control of our universe, where every moment is a wonderful, wonderful moment, it is impossible to be unhappy. And I say that

The Power of Love

is our natural state when these negative feelings are released.

Some day you are going to do it. You are in the same boat where you are struggling, and you're doing everything to achieve that happiness, and some day you are going to get it because you will never stop until you get there. But if you want to do it faster, do it our way. I promise you will be very pleasantly surprised. Everything you are looking for is right where you are. All you need to do is to take off the blinders. Your vision is very blurred. You're looking through these subconscious programs—when you release them, your vision becomes clear and you discover you are the greatest. You're whole, you're complete, you're eternal. All your fear of dying disappears. And life is so comfortable after that, and there is no struggle, no struggle whatsoever, when you get these negative feelings up and out.

So I urge you to learn this technique. It's a tool, and in one week's time, there will be a big change in you for the better, and from there on, you will continue to

The Power of Love

get better and better, lighter and lighter, happier and happier.

This thing called love is your basic nature. All the love in the universe is in your basic nature. You will discover that happiness—your happiness—equates to your capacity to love, and conversely all your miseries equate to your need to be loved. Just love, love, love and you will be so happy and healthy and prosperous. But again, you need to lift out the non-love feelings. So again I urge you to try our way. I promise that you will be very satisfied. Try it, you will like it. Thank you so much for coming.

A few more words from

Lester Levenson

The Power of Love

A MESSAGE FROM LESTER

So we have had a chance to talk heart to heart. I hope this has helped you. And I want you to know there is much more help available. I have talked to you in a manner that is designed to provoke thinking that leads you to a new realization. I have talked to you in a way that attempts to reach the part of you that inherently and intuitively understands more than your intellect. All this leads you to wisdom. Wisdom that is higher than intellectual knowledge.

If you have found these words of value, I suggest you go on and explore the do-it-yourself method I have developed that will show you how to increase your understanding every day. It is called the Release® Technique. It will give you keys to self-growth and allow you to keep it going from here on. The Release Technique is based on the premise that each one of us has no limits except those that we hold onto subconsciously, and when we let go of our subconscious limitations, we discover that our potential is unlimited. Unlimited in the direction of health, happiness, affluence and materiality. The

The Power of Love

The Power of Love

Release Technique will help you achieve the kind of life you want and even more importantly, it will assist you in achieving self-realization.

The Release Technique is kind of a post-graduate course to this book. Practice it and achieve the ultimate state.

The Power of Love

APPENDIX A

LESTER'S RELEASE TECHNIQUE COURSE WILL HELP YOU

- Rid yourself of attachments and aversions.
- Feel love any time.
- Discover the truth of your being.
- Awaken to your true nature.
- Have inner transformation.
- Clear away years of accumulated confusion.
- Have abundance in every way.
- Manifest your dreams into reality.
- Rid yourself of worry.
- Access answers from your higher self.
- Have realization.

HERE'S HOW PEOPLE THAT USE LESTER'S "THE RELEASE® TECHNIQUE" HAVE MORE ABUNDANCE WITH EASE

"The most pronounced, tangible evidence that I'm getting, only through using the method, is in the monetary aspects of my business. I'm on a commission basis only, and I've earned as much in the first quarter of this year as I did in all of last year."

Karen Brock, Woodland Hills, CA
President, Brock Enterprises

"I took The Release Technique because I was under a lot of business and personal pressure. I find now that I'm more relaxed, easier in all my relationships and making a lot more money with much less effort—playing smarter, not harder."

Tom Beyers, Scottsdale, AZ
Senior Vice President, First Federal Mortgage Company

"My business has tripled since learning the Abundance Course, yet I'm spending most of my time traveling and having fun all the time. The Technique is so powerful, I've had my entire family learn the Technique. I also got rid of 20 years of asthma. Last month I made over 1 million dollars using this Technique."

Jim Whitman, World Traveler

"I have regained my focus on abundance thanks to The Abundance Course. Customers are calling me to advertise on my radio show—big time! I recommend it to all who want abundance, riches, success, happiness and health. It really does work."

Jacquie Solomon, Phoenix, AZ
Radio Hostess, KFNX

"I'm excited!" I have already made over $7,000 and I am working on a deal now I expect to triple that...Anyone can do it. All that the Abundance course claims is true and then some. I can't imagine everyone not taking this course."

Kathy Shoden, Los Angeles, CA
Sales and Marketing

"I just completed the Abundance Course for the first time last weekend. On the second day, I received an offer for a house I have been trying to sell for three years. Before the course ended, I received three offers on the house. My sales results have been amazing—I've had the biggest month I ever had, and that's just in one week! I can't imagine anyone not wanting to learn The Easy Way."

Gayle Henderson, Scottsdale, AZ
Russ Lyon Realty Co.

VAST ABUNDANCE IS WITHIN YOU... WHY NOT JOIN IN ON THE FUN?

HAVE ABUNDANT HEALTH

"I took the Abundance Course to have more financial abundance in my life. Not only did I get that big time, but I had chronic pain in my jaw for 6 years. I was able to get rid of it the very first evening of practicing The Technique. My golf improved, I lowered my score by 14 points in two weeks. This course is worth millions—Don't wait. Call them right now!"

Roger Brunnetti, Woodland Hills, CA
Marketing Consultant

I have had a full recovery from a boating accident since taking the course. I did not have full range-of-motion in my left arm, I do now and I have been able to stop taking 14 different pills."

Raul Marmol, Claremont, CA

"During the second day, I worked on an injured foot that had been bothering me for years. I was wearing a bandage and a sandal. The next day I was able to wear shoes and it didn't hurt me at all! I'm not angry at anyone, and I like myself more, and I feel joy all the time. Wow!"

Cathryn Willmeng, Phoenix, AZ
Real Estate Appraiser

"I let go of a lower back pain I had been suffering with for a long time during the third day of the course. I even took off my back support—WOW, what a course."

Gary Sylvester, San Diego, CA
Telecommunications

BE IN TOTAL CONTROL OF YOUR LIFE

"On Sunday morning (during the course), I woke up with the knowledge that I had found the tools that empower me to take back control of my life, and that's not a goal—that's a fact."

Linda Carella, Los Angeles, CA
V.P. Marketing, Tova Corp.

"Acceptance expanded, trust expanded, love expanded, freedom is and continuously unfolds easily! I also received five checks in the mail yesterday—and money and joy just keep rolling in. I also have a major art show this week at the Scottsdale Art Center and it just happened with ease."

Monica Martinez, Phoenix, AZ
artist

"This course helped me bring back the value of more consistent releasing. It has given me the awareness to use the tools I have for releasing with ease. Thank you for putting such a practical spin on the method. My life is so much richer for having use of the tools and Lester's wisdom."

Rosalie Lurie, Los Angeles, CA, Fundraiser

"I no longer judge myself and others. I no longer feel guilty about anything; I love myself and others. I'm experiencing peace and joy more and more. I can't imagine anyone not taking this fabulous course."

Scott Jones, Mission Viejo, CA
Advertising Executive

"I gained the ability to stop being counterproductive in my life. I can now erase any attitude of 'I never win.' It enabled me to take control of myself—wow!"

Kathy Mullen, El Segundo, CA

RID YOURSELF OF FAILURE HABITS

"I actually let go of beating myself up—I hadn't thought it was possible. I feel exhilarated and energetic after years of fatigue. I have more clarity and peace and improved self confidence—I have a feeling of 'I can' after years of depressions and anxiety—Thank you Lester and Larry."

Luz Ugalde Fortner, Ventura, CA

"I've taken many lessons, but it wasn't until I took The Release Technique that I really, really got on track. Wow–I really didn't know what I was missing! Releasing is the greatest, and our natural way...Don't miss this opportunity."

Ron Hamady, Los Angeles, CA, Movie Producer

RID YOURSELF OF FEAR AND GAIN CLARITY

I unlocked my fear, lack and scarcity feelings that stopped me from having abundance for years. It was powerful and fun and easy. I can't imagine anyone not taking this course—it's a must."

Joseph Harrington, Los Angeles, Ca
Psychologist

"My clarity in life improved dramatically. I see where I am and where to go next. My abundance improved just in that one weekend—I wish all could attend."

Craig Davis, Winnetka, CA, School Psychologist

"I had severe anxiety when I would get on the freeway. It was preventing me from having a life. Then I took The Abundance Course. On the first day, I dumped the phobia. It was so simple that it was almost hard to believe it could be so easy! I now look at life in such a way that it becomes magical. I recommend it to all."

Lauren Brent, Los Angeles, CA
Esthetician

"I was able to retire from a job I had for years, and I feel terrific about it! I'm using the 'Butt' system and it works. Thank you, the course is the greatest."

Charles Jones, Washington, DC
Psychotherapist

"I released about worrying about the future. My life really works!"

Bebe Young, Paramount, CA
Businesswoman

"I just completed The Abundance Course. My understanding gets clearer and clearer. My decision process is fantastic, and I'm having fun all the time. My business has tripled, and I have more time to do what I want. It's easy—anyone can do it."

Judy Smith Whitman, Scottsdale, AZ
Art Dealer

FEEL LOVE ANYTIME YOU WANT

"These past few weeks have been especially wonderful—'Joyous' is the true word. More and more I do see myself as one with everything. Right now, Larry, I feel as if I'm going to explode with joy—and I can't stop laughing! All is well! All should join in on the fun."

Clara Sida-McCoy, Glendale, AZ
Housewife/Secretary

"The new work that is being done on abundance is fantastic. I'm just busting with happiness and doing and having what I want all the time."

Cecilia Gallagher, Scottsdale, AZ
Business Developer

"I never thought I could feel this good about myself. I now have a tool I can use each day of my life."

Yvonne Medina, Los Angeles, CA
Client Service Genetics Institute

UNLOCK WHAT'S HOLDING YOU BACK FROM HAVING TOTAL ABUNDANCE AND JOY IN YOUR LIFE—ONCE AND FOR ALL LEARN TO TRUST YOURSELF

"By the end of Day 2, I achieved a sense of deep calm. While driving home, I found I wasn't so irritated by other drivers and I remained unperturbed. My boyfriend commented on the youthful, lighter look on my face over dinner."

Kim LaChance, Lawndale, CA
Therapist

"I have been going through books and seminars for so long. This course allowed me to see that life can be without problems. The future is wonderful now."

Pirayeh Shaban, Pasadena, CA
Coordinator

IMPROVE RELATIONSHIPS

"I am able to release my anger at my girlfriend whenever she gets angry/jealous about our relationship. Our relationship has greatly improved in a short time."

Jay Torres, Culver City, CA
Salesman

"My relationship with my children has greatly improved. I am able to handle disgruntled clients without being uptight. I lost my craving for smoking and stopped smoking in the first day of the course."

Thomas Mitchel, Los Angeles, CA
Investment Advisor

"Everything is working for me with ease—my relationships are getting better, my business is exploding with ease, abundance just is and it's easy!"

Shawna Leach-Lugo, Phoenix, AZ
Artist

"I can allow myself to love people for who they are, no matter what."

John Cullen, Lake-in-the-Hills, IL
Contractor

MORE REPORTS FROM ABUNDANCE COURSE GRADUATES WHO HAVE DROPPED UNWANTED HABITS

"A few weeks after learning The Release Technique, I completely stopped my chain smoking habit and the craving hasn't come back in 15 years since stopping."

Don Janklow, Westlake Village, CA
President, Janklow & Associates

"I have learned to relax by releasing, and an unexpected gain has been that I no longer have a desire for alcohol—it feels good."

Jack Dimalante, New York

"I lost five pounds during the first week of the course without thinking about it!"

Lloyd Scott, Dallas, TX

"I used this method when I was feeling hunger, and I no longer feel the desire to eat."

Rita Recken, Glandorf, OH

ELIMINATE STRESS

"Sleeping better than I have in years. I quit taking drugs for my arthritis and feel better without them."

Raymond Hanson, Los Angeles, CA

"I connected with the ease of releasing. I simply didn't know how much resistance I had. By Sunday, I had so much energy it was great and after only four hours of sleep. I feel lighter and happier."

Ariana Attie, Los Angeles, CA, Legal Secretary

"The first weekend I discovered my feeling of fatigue could be alleviated, and I drove 200 miles without the sleepiness and feeling of heaviness that so often plagued me."

Ruth A. Riegel, Chicago, IL

"I had several physical ailments including migraine headaches, diverticulitis, gout and severe hypoglycemia, and the week after taking the course was scheduled for surgery. But within a few days after beginning to release, the surgical condition disappeared and never re-appeared. My other physical problems cleared up. I believe these good effects are due to the stress reduction brought about by using the Method."

Dr. David Hawkins, Manhasset, NY
Medical Director, The North Nassau Mental Health Center

"I think it is becoming evident, in my observation, that the techniques learned in the program were beneficial to people who work under the stress and strain that we do in the Investment Banking Industry. I have personally benefited, especially when I ran the New York City Marathon shortly after an illness."

Thomas J. Kitrick
Vice President Training and Development, Goldman, Sachs & Co.

40-YEAR SEARCH IS OVER

"Over the last 40 years, I have spent thousands of dollars and invested hundreds of hours in an uncountable number of seminars, courses and techniques. I purchased The Abundance Course hoping, as always, that I had finally found something that would work. I did! Now my reactions to events during the day are much more positive than ever before. Wow!"

Bill Cook, Norman, OK

MULTIMILLIONAIRE HEALS HEART

"I am a multimillionaire who has learned how to attract money easily into my life via the route to real estate development. What I had not known was that it is okay to enjoy my work and it is okay to enjoy spending the fruits of my labor. I am now able to tithe and gift and spend my money joyfully and peacefully. What a difference The Abundance Course made in this miraculous turnaround of attitude for me. Further, my heart used to hurt and the doctors would consistently tell me it is fine. My heart no longer hurts me–I've released, it's free."

Robert White, Boston, MA

TRIPLES INCOME

"Thank you for your wonderful "Abundance" tapes. After listening to your tapes a thought popped into my mind that increased my income 3 times. I evaluate children (I'm a consulting school psychologist) at a rate of $350/evaluation–write up reports and type them on a computer–formerly one evaluation a day. I now do three evaluations (takes 1 1/2 hrs. per evaluation), tape my reports and have the school secretary type them up. My income is now over $1,000/day and I work only 2 days a week. I have more leisure time to do other things that give me joy. Again, thanks to you and the works of Lester Levenson–a truly great man. "

Dr. Samuel L. Beitchman, Ph.D., Mount Laurel, NJ

JOY SPILLING OUT

"The Abundance Course is truly the marvel of life. I am a skeptical person (or I was!) and I didn't think the course would do much for me, but now I am a believer—actually I know that this course is the key to happiness with no sorrow. Right now, I feel absolutely joyous—it's spilling out of me—and it's for the best reason, which is no reason at all.

I'd like to thank you for your everlasting patience, love and givingness that Lester shared with us."

Foster Brown, Massachusetts

HAPPY ALL THE TIME AND MAKES $100,000 IN ONE WEEK

"The Abundance Course just got me much clearer about my life. It showed me how to have a positive attitude all the time. I'm now happy all the time and the joy is just bubbling up. Because I'm even so much more positive now, I was able to make $100,000 last week in the stock market."

Sarit Majhor, Sante Fe, NM

HAPPIEST TIME IN HIS ENTIRE LIFE

"After ordering and receiving the home study version of The Abundance Course, I allowed it to sit on the shelf for several months. Then one day I simply decided to follow the instructions and do it on a daily basis. That was about 3 months ago, and what a journey it has been. Traditionally my medical practice slows down the first quarter of the year for various reasons and picks up in the spring. Amazingly, I have had the most productive January I've had in many years, and continues into February. In fact, January was the second most productive month I have had in twelve months. Not only that, something in a profound way has happened to my attitude toward my patients and life in general. I feel so much love toward my patients and about everyone else. It's really weird. I have come to the conclusion that I just may be the happiest I have ever been in my entire life. That's not bad for a person who previously thought he was just an old, worn-out Doc."

Dr. Clyde Shreve, Ogden, UT

ONENESS AND BLISS

"I cannot express the extent of my gratitude for the wisdom you imparted to me this past weekend. The Abundance Course was beyond anything I could have imagined– indeed it finally gave me an experience that I had been searching for 19 years. I picked up a book on Zen Buddhism at the time I have been searching for the experience described in that book and the many, many others I have read since that time. I have tried various techniques since that time including intensive medication, Tony Robbins, etc. but it wasn't until I was driving home from The Abundance Course (driving down a Los Angeles freeway no less) that I had an experience of Oneness and Bliss. I finally have found the way out of the feeling of separateness and pain that comes with living a normal human life. This is priceless knowledge and timeless wisdom."

Sonny Ritscher, Los Angeles, CA

OVERCOMES SADNESS EASILY

"In September 1994, my youngest son, Matt, age 21, was killed in an auto accident and for these seven years I lived in grief. Though the pain eased over the years I could hardly speak his name without breaking down. I completed The Abundance Course at the end of October and last week released on Matt's death. I felt like someone had lifted a boulder off my back. The empty, squeezing, tightness in my chest was gone. I felt wonderful, so to see how much I'd release I watched a home video. Seeing Matt I felt only love and happiness. (No more tears, no more pain.) Yesterday I even talked to a friend about the accident and did not get upset in the least. This is a tremendous gain for me and I recommend this course to everyone.

Thank you so much!"

Jeri Von Wolff, West Des Moines, IA

M.D.'S HEALTH IMPROVES

"My allergies have improved significantly since using The Abundance Course. I used to have really bad neck and back tension and that has improved significantly as well. I am more at peace with regard to my relationships with my parents. My ability to treat patients has improved and I feel better able to tune-in with what's going on with others. I recommend the course to anyone who wants to improve their life in every way."

Clara Hsu, M.D., Los Angeles, CA

Learn Lester's Abundance Course!

Now on audio, personally recorded by Lester Levenson and Larry Crane

Lester Levenson

This new, exciting and professionally produced twenty-session audio series has all of Lester's material that will help you go all the way and have abundance of everything in life. The perfect way for you to achieve a whole new level in conscious and master your life.

I have kept in contact with many of the graduates who have personally used these audios. THE RESULTS HAVE BEEN PHENOMENAL. The momentum has been wonderful and it's spreading. IT IS MY INTENT TO HAVE YOU LEARN THESE ADVANCED TECHNIQUES AND FULLY KNOW WHAT LESTER KNOWS. At the core of this course is the magic Lester brought to the subject of attachments and aversions. I have taken these simple, practical and remarkable tools and created this Abundance Course. By using this audio series, you will eliminate the blocks that are stopping you from having complete freedom in your life. I recently completed a remarkable new audio program that brings Lester's course to you in the comfort and privacy of your own home, or anywhere you play audios.

And, having these audios in your possession is like having an instructor at our beck and call. Anytime you want an instructor to help you, just pop an audio into your player! You will sit back and watch your limitations just fly out. You'll have the opportunity to work on issues that are important to you and you'll learn more about The Technique as you listen to me guide you through the experience, JUST AS LESTER TAUGHT ME.

Here's What You'll Get

- You'll receive 20 audio sessions of ten "How to do it" Abundance Course audios that will change your life forever.
- You will learn in the privacy of your home how to eliminate any and all of life's burdens and obstacles that are in the way of getting what you truly want in life, fast.
- These 20 audio sessions will take you to a place where you will experience total abundance, peace of mind, health and unlimited happiness.
- You'll discover Lester's secret and discover for yourself why it works for you.
- You'll receive a workbook showing you how to use Lester's *No Attachments, No Aversions Course.*
- Yours **FREE!** Order right now or within the next 5 days and we will give you **THREE FREE BONUS AUDIOs VALUED AT $65.** You'll receive the "In My Own Words" audio in which Lester describes his own personal tips to that natural state he called "happiness with no sorrow." And, as a second bonus, you will receive a special audio called "Will Power." In this audio Lester shares the secret to willing things to happen. The third bonus audio is called "Beingness." It takes you to that place that Lester describes.

Don't forget, the solution is available and it's yours for the taking. I know the difference it will make in your life and what it will mean to your family and loved ones, too. Lastly, may I ask you something? How quickly and easily would you travel if all the burdens you are carrying were removed from your back?

It's so simple. Can you picture it? I know you can.

If you have any questions please don't hesitate to call me 1-888-333-7703. I truly want to make every effort I can to share with you the way to a life of abundance, peace of mind, health and happiness.

Sincerely,

Larry Crane

Larry Crane

The Abundance Course audio series includes 20 sessions of ten "How to Do It" Abundance Course audios in two beautiful vinyl albums with an accompanying workbook—plus:

Three **FREE** bonus audios. All this is yours for only $199* plus $12.95 U.S. shipping and handling. We are making a limited quantity of this set available to seekers and their friends at this special price. Orders will be filled on a first come first served basis, so order yours today. Call toll-free 1-888-333-7703 or mail a check, made out to Lawrence Crane Enterprises, Inc., to:

Lawrence Crane Enterprises, Inc.
2800 Crusader Circle, Suite 10, Virginia Beach, VA 23453

Outside the U.S. call:
818-385-0611
From Canada call toll-free:
877-472-3317
Fax: 818-385-0563
Email: releasela@aol.com
or visit our Web site:
www.releaseTechnique.com
All credit cards are accepted.

*California residents please add 8.25% sales tax.

You Save $199 —NOW!*

Save $200 *over* *for a limited time*

☐ **Yes!** Please rush me the **Abundance Course** Home Study audio set so I may examine it risk-free for 30 days.

☐ **Yes!** I read THE POWER OF LOVE BOOK, so I qualify for the specialprice of $199. I save $136 off the regular price of $335.

☐ **Yes!** I also qualify for the **3 free audios**, a $65 value, mine to keep even if I return the material for a full refund.
(Less shipping and handling, of course.)

☐ Please rush me **audio cassettes**.   ☐ Please rush me **CDs**.

☐ Enclosed is $211.95 ($199 plus $12.95 U.S. for shipping and handling)
(Overseas orders $246.95 U.S.—$199 plus $47.95 shipping and handling)
CA residents please add $16.41 (8.25%) sales tax. Total = $228.36
Sorry, we do not accept C.O.D. orders.
Make checks payable to Lawrence Crane Enterprises, Inc.

Total _____   ☐ Check ☐ Visa ☐ MasterCard

Your discount code is POL1.   ☐ Discover ☐ American Express

For fast action, call toll-free (24 hours a day): 1-888-333-7703

Name _____

Address _____ City _____ State ____ Zip _____

Phone (day) _____ (eve.) _____
(In case we need to contact you if there is a question about your order.)

E-mail _____ Occupation _____

Credit Card # _____ Expiration Date _____

Signature _____
Please be sure to check your address carefully and indicate any corrections.

The Release Technique
2800 Crusader Circle, Suite 10, Virginia Beach, VA 23453

DOUBLE GUARANTEE

*If I am not convinced that the Abundance Course will work for me I may:
1) Receive Free coaching over the telephone, or 2) Return the course within 30 days for a prompt refund and still keep the 3 free bonus audios.*
(Less shipping and handling, of course.)

No Attachments, No Aversions

The Autobiography of a Master

by Lester Levenson

Lester tells his own story in his very own words. In the margin are Lester's own notes in his own handwriting. Each time you read it you will discover something profound that will help you in your own personal quest towards freedom.

"For the first time, a living American Master tells the story of his life and details step by step in simple, everyday English how he achieved the extraordinary powers of omniscience, omnipresence, and omnipotence.

This twentieth century Master came into his immortality not by the shores of the Ganges, nor on the heights of the Himalayas, but in the bustling heart of New York City.

Lester Levenson—born in New Jersey, a former physicist and businessman—points the way to freedom that Westerners can readily understand and follow."

Larry Crane

Lawrence Crane
Author and teacher of Lester's "Release Technique"

The cost is $25 plus $5 shipping and handling. Total: $30. Item #1012
(California residents please add $2.50 [8.25% sales tax] for a total of $32.50.)
Call 888-333-7703 to order
Make check payable to: Lawrence Crane Enterprises
Mail to:, Lawrence Crane Enterprises, Inc.
2800 Crusader Circle, Suite 10, Virginia Beach, VA 23453

The Ultimate Truth
About Love & Happiness
A Handbook to Life

The Ultimate Truth is Truth that is true now, has always been true, and will forever be true.

Man cannot make this Truth nor can he change this Truth. He can only discover it. He may choose to live in accord with it. If he so does, he finds himself supremely happy beyond anything he could imagine! All limitations drop away and he discovers that all power, all knowledge, and all joy are his and that all this is his natural, inherent state.

A unique characteristic of this Truth is that it must be seen by each one through his own perception. No one and no book can do it for him. Teachers and books (scriptures) can only point out the direction, the way, and the individual may choose to take it.

Necessary is the proof of Truth, and necessary it is that each one must prove the Truth for himself. Nothing should ever be accepted on hearsay. One should listen to, reflect upon, and then prove. The best attitude one may take would be to not believe nor disbelieve, but to accept Truths for checking. Then, and only then, after one has proven them without a doubt should one accept them.

As Truth begins to prove itself, one gains more confidence in it, and then proofs come more easily and more readily; until finally, one perceives the Absolute Truth—that we are unlimited beings, unlimited in our knowledge, power and joy.

The cost is $20 plus $5 shipping and handling. Total: $25. Item #1011
Call 888-333-7703 to order

Make check payable to: Lawrence Crane Enterprises

Mail to:, Lawrence Crane Enterprises, Inc.
2800 Crusader Circle, Suite 10, Virginia Beach, VA 23453

Books and Audios from Lester Levenson

The Ultimate Truth
Book by Lester Levenson
> Lester discusses subjects like: Happiness, love, truth, peace, the ego, the mind, the world, sex and marriage, pleasure-pain, health and supply, spiritual growth, self-growth yardsticks. A brand new book.

Item #1011 $20.00 plus $5.00 shipping*

No Attachments, No Aversions
The Autobiography of a Master—book
> Lester tells his own story in his very own words. In the margin are Lester's own notes in his own handwriting. Each time you read it you will discover something profound that will help you in your own personal quest toward freedom.

Item #1012 $25.00 plus $5.00 shipping*

In Retreat with Lester Levenson
Audios
> This dynamic three-audio set of Lester Levenson was recorded live at several Nine-Day Retreats in the 1980s. These audios are full of practical suggestions on how to accelerate your releasing for freedom. They also contain rare accounts of Lester describing his personal experience of freedom.

Item #1007-T/#1007-CD $39.95 plus $6.00 shipping*

The Way with Lester Levenson
Audios
> Three audio programs of Lester Levenson recorded in 1989. Lester was pulling no punches as he spoke with a small, dedicated group of staff at the Retreat Center. These rare recordings contain powerful pointers on how to achieve freedom now. This three audio set includes a bonus audio recorded in 1973.

Item #1006-T/#1006-CD $39.95 plus $6.00 shipping*

The Ultimate Goal—Volume I
in Lester's Own Words—Audios
> Audio 1 —The Ultimate Truth; Experiencing Truth
> Audio 2—Letting Go of Ego
> Audio 3—The Mind Mirror
> Audio 4—Creating All You Desire
> Audio 5—Silence, Love and Grace
> Audio 6—The Key to Individual Freedom

Item #1005-T #1005-CD $79.95 plus $8.00 shipping*

A Fireside Chat with Lester Levenson
Audios

We all have many questions that we would love to ask Lester. Hear Lester answering puzzling questions from graduates.
Audio 1—Looking for Happiness
Audio 2—Attachments and Aversions
Audio 3—Communication and Love
Audio 4—About Releasing
Item #1024-T / #1024-CD $39.95 plus $6.00 shipping*

The Ultimate Goal–Volume II
Lester on Audios

Audio 1—Happiness is Love
Audio 2—The Source of All Intelligence
Audio 3—The Answer is Here All the Time
Audio 4—There Are No Problems
Audio 5—The Steps to Being What You Are
Audio 6—Beingness
Item #1008-T / #1008-CD $79.95 plus $8.00 shipping*

The Abundance Book
Comes with 2 bonus audios

The Abundance Course has now been published in book form. It's a terrific way to Supercharge your Releasing skills.

This Exciting Book Will Help You:
- Reinforce and Supercharge your Releasing
- Have long-term financial success
- Deal calmly with world events regardless of what the media says
- Have inner calmness in the midst of pressure
- Propel yourself to new heights of joy and fulfillment
- Have vibrant health and energy

Item #1015T / #1015-CD $65 plus $12.95 shipping*

How to Order Today

CA residents please add sales tax (8.25%).

Order by Phone:
1-888-333-7703 Toll-free (24 hours a day)
Outside U.S. call 1-541-957-4969
Toll-free Canada, Hawaii, Alaska: 1-877-472-3317

Order by Fax:
1-757-301-3646

Order by Mail:
Lawrence Crane Enterprises, Inc.
2800 Crusader Circle, Suite 10
Virginia Beach, VA 23453

Order from our Secure Web Site:
www.releaseTechnique.com

All Credit Cards Accepted